Original title:
A Garland of Christmas Dreams

Copyright © 2024 Creative Arts Management OÜ
All rights reserved.

Author: Harrison Blake
ISBN HARDBACK: 978-9916-94-102-7
ISBN PAPERBACK: 978-9916-94-103-4

Nighttime Stories of Yuletide Magic

In a snowy town where reindeer roam,
Santa lost his way back home.
He took a sleigh ride with the cat,
Now that's a sight, imagine that!

Elves dance wildly on the roof,
Tripping over every hoof.
With tinsel tangled in their hair,
They chuckle loud, without a care.

Cookies disappear in a flash,
While the milk's turnin' into a splash.
Rudolph giggles, tells a tale,
Of a penguin who tried to sail!

Jingle bells ring with goofy glee,
As snowflakes fall, so joyfully.
Join in the fun, let laughter rise,
Underneath the twinkling skies!

Hushed Melodies of the Winter Night

Snowmen wearing hats so tall,
A penguin takes a winter fall.
Sleds fly by with goofy grace,
While cocoa spills in every place.

Frothy mugs and marshmallow fights,
Frosty noses, oh what sights!
Elves are dancing in a heap,
As winter whispers, secrets keep.

Sparkling Eyes and Twinkling Hearts

Socks stuffed with candy, oh what bliss,
Chocolate treats we can't dismiss.
Giggling kids in reindeer gear,
Stealing snacks when no one's near.

Glittering lights on every street,
A cat that thinks it's all a treat!
Tinsel tangled in the tree,
What's that noise? It's just a bee!

Echoes of Laughter in Snowy Light

Snowball fights that end in laughs,
Sledding down the icy paths.
Chasing shadows through the night,
Underneath the soft moonlight.

Giggles echo on the breeze,
Falling snowflakes, aims to please.
Whiskers twitch from cute old dogs,
While everyone poses like odd logs.

A Symphony of Joyous Revelry

Singing songs round fireside cheer,
Where grandma's dance has no fear.
Cooky crumbs on noses bright,
As we munch through a winter night.

Jingle bells with silly tunes,
Blasting carols 'til the moons.
Funky hats and bright red bows,
Who knew laughter brightly glows?

Enchanted Nights Wrapped in Warmth

Snowmen dance, their noses bright,
Jingle bells ring with pure delight.
Hot cocoa spills, a marshmallow fight,
In fuzzy socks, we glow at night.

Elves in pajamas, they can't be seen,
Hiding snacks where they've never been.
Cookies vanish, it's quite the scene,
As reindeer giggle and munch on greens.

Boughs of Fir the Hold Our Dreams

Tinsel twinkles like stars above,
While cat naps underneath, oh how they shove.
Scent of pine mixed with sweet love,
A squirrel steals a bauble, those brats, they shove.

Ornaments swapped for rubber ducks,
Each shiny ball, our festive luck.
Grandma giggles, 'She took my brooks!'
As snow falls softly, we share our chuck.

The Glow of Friendship by the Fireside

Friendship glows like a cozy fire,
Where jokes are told, and dreams conspire.
We roast marshmallows, and laughter's dire,
Fuzzy slippers and fashion choice, dire!

Stockings stuffed full of silly treats,
Giant-sized mittens for goofy feats.
With friends beside, the heart repeats,
Holiday laughter that never depletes.

Dreaming in Glimmering Winter Light

Outside it's frosty, but we're all warm,
Wrapped in blankets, each one a charm.
We giggle 'bout snowstorms, causing alarm,
And plot silly games, oh they're a swarm.

Icicles glisten, but we've got flair,
With fuzzy hats and mismatched pairs.
Walking in snow, life's full of cares,
While we chase snowflakes, no one compares.

Sprigs of Joy in the Snow

Tiny snowflakes dance as we play,
Frosty noses laugh, it's a merry fray.
Snowmen wobble, hats fall down,
Their button eyes can't hide a frown.

With every slip, a giggle ensues,
Hot cocoa dreams wrapped in cozy hues.
Snowball fights morph into wild chases,
Joy in the air, all smiling faces.

The Sleigh Ride of Wishes

Ho ho ho, the sleigh takes flight,
Reindeer prance in the moon's soft light.
Filled with toys and tasty treats,
Bouncing laughter, quick merry beats.

Oops! A bump, we hit a tree,
Santa's hoot echoes, full of glee.
Lists were wrong, oh what a blunder,
We've brought back a dog that loves to thunder!

Memories Wrapped in Ribbon

Under the tree, the gifts do tease,
Tangled lights make us giggle with ease.
Grandma's fruitcake, a mystery to share,
Unwraps more laughter than flavors rare.

Cats in boxes, oh what a sight,
Playing pounce till the early night.
Squirrels nibble on ribbons bright,
Can't stop chuckling at their delight.

Celestial Crystals of the Season

Icicles shimmer like festive grin,
Frosted windows tell tales within.
Elves on shelves with their goofy poses,
Toasting marshmallows, their noses do roses.

Mystery socks slip into the night,
Mismatched pairs taking off in flight.
Giggles echo through crisp, starry skies,
Whispers of cheer, where magic lies.

Candles Flicker in Silent Prayers

Candles flicker, oh what a sight,
Cats chase shadows, with all their might.
Grandma's knitting flies everywhere,
Mittens end up tangled in her hair.

A turkey dances, sings a sweet tune,
While Uncle Bob hoots, wearing a spoon.
The dog steals the pie, a sly little thief,
Everyone laughs, beneath their disbelief.

Whispering Pines in a Snowy Veil

Whispering pines, with secrets to share,
Snowballs are thrown, flying through the air.
Sleds belly flop down snowy hills,
Falling in giggles, just gives us chills.

A snowman wobbles, eyes made of coal,
Waving a carrot, bold as a troll.
Penguins in snow boots, oh what a sight,
Dance alongside the stars, in the frostbitten night.

Woven Dreams of Comfort and Cheer

Woven dreams with tinsel and glee,
Peppermint dances in hot cocoa spree.
Elf hats are floppy, some too big to wear,
Laughter erupts like bubbles in air.

The fruitcake's singing, it thinks it's a star,
Kerfuffle ensues, it rolls off the bar.
Sprinkle some jingles, a dash of delight,
In this merry whirlwind, we take flight.

Celestial Glow of Winter's Embrace

Celestial glow on this frosty night,
Jingle bells echo, what a delight!
Socks mismatched, we wander around,
Chasing lost presents that never were found.

The reindeer are snoring, taking a break,
While cookies are munching, oh what a quake.
Midnight mischief, we toast with a cheer,
For all of these moments, we hold dear.

Sweet Tidings of Midnight Wishes

In the night, the cats all sing,
Chasing mice, oh, what a fling!
Santa trips on candy canes,
While the reindeer dance with sprains.

Snowmen giggle, hats askew,
Hot cocoa spills, a tasty brew!
Kids toss snowballs with delight,
As parents nap, tucked in tight.

Seasons of Warmth and Wonder

Grandma's cookies, burnt just right,
Smoke alarms blare, what a sight!
Jingle bells on puppy's collar,
Whispers of the kids' loud holler.

Mittens lost and socks that squeak,
Laughter echoes, voices peek.
The tree is dressed in tinsel bright,
Unruly cats cause such a fright.

Enchanted Evenings Under the Stars

Sipping cider, mustache of foam,
Gifts wrapped up, a rolling gnome!
Chasing shadows in the moon,
While dad sings a silly tune.

Frosty faces wearing grins,
Turkey's gone, oh where's it been?
Santa sneezes, reindeer pounce,
In the snow, they all announce!

Frosted Dreams and Flickering Flames

Candles flicker, shadows dance,
Uncles prance in bright expanse!
Fruitcake bounces off the wall,
While the dog just takes the fall.

Gingerbread men, who knew they'd flee?
Hiding fast behind the tree.
Snowflakes fall, they kiss our noses,
In this mayhem, joy just growses!

Wishes Danced on Candlelight

In cozy nooks, our wishes twirl,
Like little elves in a fizzy whirl.
With mistletoe stuck on a cat's head,
We're laughing so hard, we might fall dead.

Cookies gone missing, the milk's all gone,
The secret is out, blame it on Ron!
A sprinkle of giggles, a dash of cheer,
We've got enough joy to last through the year.

The Soft Embrace of December

Snowflakes tickle like tiny feet,
They dance around in a snowy sheet.
Grandpa's on skates, he's lost his grace,
Spinning and wobbling all over the place.

The tree's decked out with socks and ties,
With lights that sparkle like starry skies.
And if you peek close, you might just see,
A squirrel trying to sip on hot tea!

Threads of Cheer in Winter's Loom

With yarn and laughter, we stitch the night,
Creating a scene that's quite the sight.
The cat's in the stocking, purring a tune,
While the dog plays fetch with the Christmas moon.

A gingerbread house that's wobbly-built,
Fell over again, oh what a guilt!
Whiskers in icing, surprise in return,
These festive blunders, oh how we yearn!

Frost-Kissed Mornings of Promise

Mornings are frosty, and cheer is spread,
As we trip o'er presents, then laugh instead.
The snowman's got a carrot for a nose,
But it's stuck in the snow where nobody goes!

We sip on cocoa, marshmallows afloat,
Grandma's sweater is still a bit tight, that's no joke!
With playful shivers, and giggles that soar,
We celebrate every little Winter encore!

Dreams Wrapped in Crimson and Gold

In the attic, the stockings sag,
With toys that dance and rattlesnag.
Santa tripped on the cat again,
Oh dear, what a festive pain!

Chubby cheeks and a giggle spree,
Dancing round the Christmas tree.
Hot cocoa spills with each wild cheer,
'Tis the season for joyful fear!

Old twinkler lights blink in delight,
While squirrels plot to steal the night.
A reindeer's laugh echoes so loud,
We wrap the cat in a red bow proud!

Snow-Drifted Tales by the Fire

Snowflakes tumble, a clumsy show,
As we slip and slide through the snow.
A snowman wobbles, head askew,
With a carrot nose that's stuck like glue.

Marshmallows roast in a fiery whirl,
As Uncle Joe gives his funny twirl.
The dog joins in, a furry mess,
Stealing socks—a holiday test!

Tales of elves, both wild and bold,
Gifts wrapped in glitter are stories told.
While laughter crackles in warm delight,
As shadows dance in the cozy light.

The Magic of Evergreen and Light

A tree stands tall, all decked with cheer,
But the cat swats at the baubles near.
Each ornament shatters, what a sight,
An evening of chaos brings great delight!

Mistletoe's up, but watch your step,
As Auntie trips, she lets out a yelp.
We all burst out laughing, snorting loud,
Together, united, a carefree crowd.

The scent of pine fills the festive air,
While silly socks adorn each stair.
Oh, the antics that fill the night,
As laughter sparkles just like the light!

Illuminated Joys of the Frosted Eve

Frosty windows, laughter so bright,
A gumdrop fight breaks out tonight.
Marshmallow missiles fly through the room,
Creating laughter, dispelling gloom.

Cake crumbs spread, a snowy bliss,
Each bite a war, we can't resist.
The dog wears a hat, quite bold and grand,
As we join together, a goofy band.

Twinkling lights form silly shapes,
While cousins dance like goofy apes.
The night is filled with joyous cheer,
In a whirl of magic, the end draws near!

Frosted Fantasies Unfurled

Snowflakes sprinkle, dance and twirl,
Elves on pogo sticks give a whirl.
The cat in stockings, sitting proud,
Presents wrapped in bubbles, not too loud.

Hot cocoa mixed with pickle juice,
A reindeer named Fred, quite the moose.
Socks that squeak with every step,
Santa's on a scooter, took a rep!

Gingerbread houses, candy glow,
While sugar rushes steal the show.
The carolers are singing loud,
Dancing rhinos make us crowd!

When morning comes, what a sight!
Toothpaste trees, a real delight.
We giggle at gifts, so bizarre,
This holiday's the best by far!

Starlit Secrets Beneath the Tree

Underneath the twinkling lights,
Squirrels are staging acorn fights.
Wrapping paper, an endless mess,
Dad in reindeer PJs, we confess.

Ornaments that laugh and grin,
Uncle Joe with eggnog on his chin.
A cat that thinks it's a gift,
Tangled lights? Just give a lift!

The tree is dancing, isn't she?
Gifts that sing in harmony.
A little robot, dancing spry,
While neighbor's snowman waves goodbye.

At night we whisper, 'What's the plan?'
To bake a cake, or maybe jam?
With cookie crumbs upon the floor,
Beneath the tree, who could ask for more?

Mistletoe Dreams in the Moonlight

Under the mistletoe, a penguin prance,
Snogging gnomes, they take a chance.
With snowman hats and a sprig or two,
   We giggle, whisper, 'What to do?'

Pine cones dressed as fancy hats,
Dancing with cats and sly little rats.
The moonlight beams, oh what a sight,
As frogs in tuxedos join the night.

A pickle ornament, all alone,
Makes us question what we've known.
A dance-off starts, the joy runs wild,
Even Santa's laughing, like a child.

Moonlit dreams of jolly cheer,
With funny quirks, dear friends draw near.
A holiday whimsy, oh what fun,
With every joke, we're happily spun!

Lanterns of Love and Light

Lanterns glow with a silly face,
Wobbling reindeer set the pace.
Snowmen wearing shades of green,
Taking selfies, it's quite the scene!

In the kitchen, chaos reigns,
Flour snowballs and silly stains.
Mom's got sprinkles in her hair,
While dad attempts a rhythmic flair.

Gifts of socks, all mismatched pairs,
Wrapping up cuddles and daft glares.
A llama dressed in tinsel shines,
With quirky joy, our laughter aligns.

At dusk we gather, lights aglow,
Silly stories begin to flow.
With every giggle, hearts take flight,
Lanterns lead us to pure delight!

A Canvas of Snowscape Dreams

Snowflakes dance like little clowns,
Dressing rooftops in fluffy gowns.
Sleds zoom by with giggling cheer,
As penguins steal the show, oh dear!

Chubby snowmen with carrot noses,
Make friends with squirrels, striking poses.
Hot cocoa spills, marshmallows dive,
In this winter, we feel alive!

Snowball fights that turn to hugs,
And Christmas lights, like happy bugs.
Elves on stilts, they prance about,
Spreading joy and silly shout!

At midnight, Santa trips on toys,
Beware, he brings more than just joys.
With giggles echoing through the night,
Even the moon can't help but smile bright!

The Heart's Lantern on Winter's Eve

Candles flicker, shadows play,
As giggling kiddos gift their sway.
Mittens paired with mismatched socks,
Catching Santa with silly knocks.

The cat outsmarts the puppy's chase,
While reindeer play a silly race.
Hot pie cooling on the sill,
A sly fox grins; what a thrill!

A tree adorned with popcorn strings,
Each bulb shines, like the laughter it brings.
While snowmen gossip, eyes aglow,
And marshmallow wars bring the show!

With each toast and funny cheer,
We ask, "Who ate the last reindeer?"
Laughter bubbles in the room,
As joy in winter starts to bloom!

Silent Halls and Merry Calls

Whispers travel through the halls,
As carolers sing with silly thralls.
Mice and cookies dance a jig,
While grandma knits a winter wig.

Jingle bells on every door,
Santa's sleigh makes a comic roar.
Tinsel tangled in the cat's fur,
Spreading giggles in a furry blur!

Nutcrackers strike a silly pose,
While granddad stumbles with his prose.
The tree leans under silly toys,
And laughter fills the hearts of boys.

As we gather, stories weave,
Of funny times that we believe.
In every knock, each joyful call,
The spirit of cheer embraces all!

Whispers of Frosted Wishes

In the meadow, snowflakes tease,
Wishes wrapped in winter breeze.
Penguins skate in silly loops,
While lumpy snowmen throw snow poops!

Frosty windows, tales unfold,
Of Santa's pants so bright and bold.
Cookies vanish near the tree,
How many left? A mystery!

Carols sung with silly flair,
While reindeer tango in midair.
In galleries of giggles bright,
Every heart ignites with light!

As we snuggle, warmth inside,
With laughter shared, there's joy and pride.
A frosty wish on every tongue,
Makes memories and dreams be sung!

Chiming Bells and Timeless Tales

Bells ring loudly, what a show,
Santa's stuck in a snowdrift, oh no!
Reindeer play poker on the roof,
While elves debate the truth of goof.

The cookies vanish, crumbs in sight,
A rogue mouse made them his delight.
Stockings hung with odd designs,
Filled with socks and old ghost vines!

Grandma's knitting, tangled and lost,
Managed to knit her own cat—what a cost!
Gifts wrapped up in colors bright,
Only to find it's last year's fright!

Snowmen chat with each other well,
Wishing they had homemade gel!
Through the night, sweet dreams do dance,
In winter's chill, all pets prance!

The Echo of Laughter in the Hearth

By the fire, laughter takes flight,
Socks on heads, what a silly sight!
Grandpa's jokes, they leap and fall,
Why did the turkey cross the hall?

A cat in a hat, it gives a meow,
As Dad dons a reindeer brow.
The hot cocoa's made with a cheer,
Tastes more like marshmallow than beer!

Chasing the dog with a broom in hand,
Makes Grandma shout, "What a fairytale land!"
The lights above blink in a race,
While fruitcake sings with a merry face!

Through the windows, the neighbors glance,
As we have our most joyful dance.
Dreams of squirrels stealing the pie,
Make us giggle and wonder why!

Pine-Scented Reveries at Dusk

The tree's all dressed in tinsel so bright,
While cats climb high for a better height.
The scent of pine wafts through the air,
As Dad tripped over the cat in despair!

Children giggle, hiding in nooks,
While searching for gifts in old storybooks.
Ornaments hang in a wobbly row,
And we debate if they're all in the flow!

Eggnog spills like a cascade of cream,
Careful, dear cousin, don't spill on the dream!
A snowball fight bursts into the room,
Turning the living space into a flume!

At dusk, as the stars start to gleam,
We peer into the chaos, it makes us beam.
The laughter echoes and memories swirl,
In this season's silly, lovely whirl!

Glistening Hopes in the Chill

In the chill of night, the lights aglow,
Grandma's cookies bring quite a show.
Snowflakes tumble, soft and white,
While Dad attempts a snowman fight!

The kids laugh loud, a flurry of glee,
Trying to catch snowflakes, oh what a spree!
As hands grow cold, noses turn pink,
Their giggles echo, we just can't blink!

Mom's sous chef dreams of a feast,
But accidentally chops up a yeast!
With flour dusting her hair like snow,
She stirs her potion to make it glow!

Presents are wrapped and stacked on the floor,
Some are gifts, and some are just lore.
In this season filled with laughter so free,
Glistening hopes swirl like a wild glee!

Starry Serenity of the Season

Snowflakes dance in silly ways,
Like penguins wearing holiday jays.
The tree's a cactus, all dressed in lights,
While squirrels plot Christmas gift fights.

Eggnog spills and cookies crumble,
As grandma's stories start to fumble.
Reindeer games on the living room floor,
Who knew they could hope for much more?

Tinsel throws and stockings fly,
A cat in a hat takes to the sky.
The stars giggle in winter's charm,
As Uncle Joe shows off his arm.

So here's to laughter, cheers, and fun,
This festive chaos has just begun!
With hugs and laughter all around,
In silly moments, joy is found.

Mistletoe Memories and Moonlight

Under the mistletoe, nobody knows,
Who'll get the kiss? Oh, the suspense grows!
The cat sits there, plotting his scheme,
While grandma's asleep, lost in a dream.

The moon shines bright in a snowy glow,
While children sneak cookies, oh, what a show!
A snowman's scarf flies off in a dash,
As neighbors all rush for the big holiday bash.

The lights flicker like a jazzy tune,
As we dance in the lounge, beneath the moon.
With every twirl, our laughter leaks,
A family tradition that boldly speaks.

Every hug that's given, every cheer that's sung,
Makes this a tale not easily flung.
As woeful carols begin to play,
We change the lyrics in a merry way.

The Heartfelt Glow of December

December brings its quirky cheer,
With snowball fights and hot cocoa near.
The lights above twinkle like stars,
While dad tries to find the keys to the car.

Socks mismatched, but that's all right,
As we try to put our tree up just right.
The ornaments are all smashed and cracked,
But they bring a smile, just like we planned.

Grandpa's snoring is louder than bells,
As we all sit and share our holiday tales.
The garland's a mess, the candles askew,
Yet joy blooms brightly in whirls of hue.

So raise your glass to the laughter inside,
A time to be silly, with loved ones beside.
As snowflakes fall, we'll dance in delight,
In this merry chaos, everything's bright.

Frosty Breath and Warmth Within

Frosty breath clouds the chilly air,
While my little brother chases the bear!
With mittens lost and sleds all stuck,
We tumble and giggle, oh, what luck!

A snow angel flops, then laughs at their fate,
While snowmen are dressed for a wintery date.
With carrot noses pointing askew,
They dance in our dreams, who knew?

Grandma's baking, oh what a mess,
Flour on faces, what's next to impress?
As pudding splats and cakes go flying,
Laughter erupts; we can't stop trying.

So here's to the fun 'neath the winter sky,
With spirits lifted, we're ready to fly.
In funny tales and warmth so sweet,
December's a blast, a joyous treat!

A Canvas Painted in Icy Beauty

In a world of snowflakes, silliness thrives,
Snowmen with carrots, such quirky vibes.
They wobble and jiggle, watch them all dance,
With a hat that's too big, they take every chance.

Ice skates are tangled, oh what a sight,
Falling and laughing, pure holiday light.
With each frozen twirl, we spin and we glide,
A slippery tale of joyous pride.

The trees dressed in tinsel, such glimmering flair,
But my cat's in the branches, with nary a care.
He swings and he sways, oh the chaos he brings,
As ornaments crash, it's a riot of bling.

Bright lights that shimmer, like stars gone awry,
Our laughter ricochets through the chilly sky.
In this winter wonderland, silly dreams bloom,
Where joy's the true theme, and fun finds its room.

Warmth Beneath a Tapestry of Snow

Under blankets we snuggle, hot cocoa in hand,
Giggling at stories, oh isn't it grand?
With marshmallows floating, sweet puffs in the brew,
While my dog wears my scarf, he thinks he's so cool.

The world outside sparkles, a flurry of cheer,
But my socks are mismatched, just look at them, dear.
As snowflakes keep falling, our games start to rise,
We build dreams from laughter and the warmest of pies.

Through frosted windows, we watch it all fall,
Snowball fights brewing, we're having a ball.
But then someone slips, arms flail in wild fright,
Now laughter erupts in the glow of our light.

As candles keep flickering, shadows take flight,
We dance in the glow, oh what a delight!
Wrapped in joy's tapestry, snug as can be,
In this warm winter haven, we're wild and we're free.

Flickering Firelight and Festive Nights

Around the young fire, we gather with glee,
Telling tales of elves, why don't they just flee?
With popcorn on strings and a kitten to chase,
The marshmallows roast with a gooey embrace.

The mantle adorned with odd little hats,
Uncle Joe's tree falls, oh wouldn't that be a blast!
The flicker of candles dances with fate,
We'll toast to our clumsiness, isn't it great?

Tinsel fight breaks out, such a glorious sight,
Wrapping ourselves in a sparkling flight.
As laughter erupts like carolers in song,
In this festive chaos, where we all belong.

With eggnog spills lurking, oh darling, beware,
We'll cherish these moments, with love in the air.
In the crackling warmth, our hearts take the lead,
As this season reminds us, it's joy that we need.

The Wish Upon a Christmas Star

As we gaze at the sky, just one twinkling light,
We wish for a pet pig that's dressed up just right.
Waddling in reindeer, with antlers so grand,
Our holiday visions are quite out of hand.

With glitter on faces, and tinsel in hair,
The star's wink is saying, 'You just can't compare!'
To the joy and the laughter that brighten our days,
As the wishes we send float in whimsical ways.

A sleigh filled with candy, oh wouldn't that thrill?
Filled to the brim, with a magical feel.
But instead we just laugh, at what could have been,
In the wishful delight where the fun never ends.

So let's all raise a glass to dreams without end,
To the wishes we make, with family and friends.
In this holiday magic, let laughter renew,
For the true gift of this season is simply us two.

Echoes of Winter's Enchantment

The snowflakes dance upon my head,
Like tiny fairies in my bread.
A snowman winks, he's got a hat,
I swear it smells like baked-up rat.

The winter wind begins to groan,
As icicles chill the garden gnome.
I slip and slide upon the street,
And land headfirst—a chilly feat!

My mittens warm, but what's the fuss?
They feel like socks made just for us.
The laughter echoes through the night,
As kids scream, "Snowball fight! Alright!"

Twinkling Lights and Silver Nights

The lights are tangled in a heap,
My cat has got them in a creep.
He thinks they're toys, those shiny blinks,
I fear he'll trip on all my drinks!

The cookies baked in festive cheer,
But burn like coal—ouch, that was near!
With frosting all in a big mess,
I slice the pie and just confess!

The carolers come with songs off-key,
They think it's magic—oh, can't you see?
Yet laughter fills the chilly air,
With goofy grins, we just don't care!

A Tapestry of Yuletide Joy

The partridge in a pear tree flies,
While Uncle Fred just eats the fries.
Christmas sweaters, oh so bright,
They stretch and groan by candlelight.

The mistletoe hangs a little low,
I duck and dodge wherever I go.
It's just a holiday so weird,
But still our family all adhered!

The table shakes with dishes stacked,
Grandma's pudding—yikes, it's cracked!
We toast with soda, yes, it's silly,
But who cares? We're all so frilly!

Frost-Kissed Hopes and Dreams

The frost on windows draws a face,
It looks like Cousin Jim; what a disgrace!
I shake my head, it's all a game,
These winter days are never the same.

Hot cocoa spills upon the floor,
I swear it was the dog's great score.
The tree's so lop-sided; what a sight,
Yet twinkling lights can make it bright!

Sledding down the hill, I scream with glee,
Till I crash into a boulder tree.
We laugh and roll like kids in snow,
These frosty days make spirits glow!

A Nocturne of Holiday Splendor

Lights twinkle on the tree, oh what a sight,
A cat in the tinsel, thanks for the fright.
Cookies piled high, like a mountain so grand,
Santa's on his way, with a sleigh and a band.

Reindeer prance with a laugh and a cheer,
While Grandpa's asleep with a drink and a beer.
Mistletoe hangs, but who'll take the chance?
Awkwardly swaying in a holiday dance.

Snowflakes fall with a sprinkle and swirl,
But a snowman's hat just made a young girl hurl.
Gifts wrapped up tight, with bows on the side,
What's that? A hamster? Oh no, it must hide!

So gather around, let the stories unfold,
From cookie catastrophes to tales of old.
Laughter and joy fill the air like a tune,
In this funny night under a silvered moon.

Echoes of Carols Through the Air

Jingle bells ringing, but who's off-key?
An elf in the corner, dear, could it be?
Singing their hearts out, with a pitch so wry,
While the puppy joins in, oh my, oh my!

Eggnog is flowing, but watch out for spills,
A plan for a toast? She just took her pills!
Chairs are all creaking, but what do they care?
As Auntie gets stuck in a festive old chair.

Baby's in the corner with wrapping galore,
But here comes the kitten, oh such a big score!
Tinsel gets tangled, the chaos ensues,
And laughter erupts like it's part of the blues.

Merry and bright, but don't lose that hat,
Because Cousin Jerry claims he's a cool cat.
With all the fun fumbles and heartfelt dismay,
Echoes of laughter make up for the fray.

Memories Cradled in Snowflakes

Children are sledding with joyous delight,
But wait! Watch that kid! Did he take a big bite?
Snowballs are flying; the battle's begun,
While Dad's in a snowdrift, oh what fun!

A snowman stands tall, but with a crooked nose,
It's wearing Dad's hat, and oh, how it glows.
Neighbors all laugh, with cocoa in hand,
While the family dog makes a dash for the sand.

Carrots for noses but where did they go?
The rabbit got hungry, stealing the show.
We'll build a new friend, all floppy and sweet,
Though the cat's got a plan for a possible treat.

On this fine holiday, with laughter so bold,
We cherish each memory, each funny retold.
Snowflakes keep falling; they dance with a swirl,
In this winter wonderland, laughter's our pearl.

Snowy Whispers of Joy and Love

Winter has come, with a blanket so bright,
But wait—someone's slipping, who turned out the lights?

Snow seems so fluffy, but hides its own tricks,
Like a hidden old toy or a pile of old bricks.

Sleds flying down hills with children and glee,
But watch for that snowman; he's plotting, you see!
With marshmallows eyeballing from whatever they find,
And the dog gets involved in the chaos, so blind.

Snowflakes are landing, like whispers from above,
Each one's a reminder of laughter and love.
Hot chocolate's brewing, let the marshies collide,
As we toast to this season and the joy we can't hide.

So gather together, with hearts all aglow,
With humor and warmth, let the good times flow.
In the snowy embrace of this festive affair,
We'll cherish the laughter, the love that we share.

Secret Wishes Beneath the Tree

Whispers float from underneath,
Socks stuffed with glee and wreath.
Candy canes in a sock,
Jingles pop like corn, tick-tock.

A cat's new toy, a ball so bright,
Rolling 'round, what a silly sight!
Grandpa's wig from years gone by,
Caught the kids with a startled cry.

Chocolate hidden in a shoe,
Who knew it could taste so blue?
A pickle tucked in a jar so neat,
Found at dawn, it's quite the treat!

Underneath, the dreams lay tight,
With giggles wrapped in pure delight.
Each wish a spark, a playful cheer,
In this jolly, silly sphere!

Starlight Dances on Frosty Leaves

Frosty leaves twirl like dancers' shoes,
Under a sky of sparkly hues.
Snowflakes waltz, oh what a show,
Twinkling bright, a frosty glow.

Little elves in a snowball fight,
Tumbling round till it feels just right.
Mittens caught on a tree branch high,
Squirrels chuckle and squirrels sigh.

Hot cocoa spills as laughter spills,
As marshmallows become winter frills.
Jumping puddles of snow and cheer,
All of nature draws us near.

Under stars, with dreams in tow,
Frosty leaves put on quite a show!
Each twinkle holds a funny tale,
Woven into winter's veil.

Enveloped in the Spirit of the Season

Around the tree, the lights go nuts,
Grandma's cookies shaped like huts.
With sprinkles flying through the air,
The kitchen's chaos beyond compare.

A snowman wearing dad's old hat,
With a carrot nose, and he looks fat.
What a sight, a real oddball,
Tipped his hat, and took a fall!

Bells are jingling with a cheer,
While the dog steals the roast so dear.
Chasing him 'round the festive feast,
A meal gone wild, to say the least!

In this wild and funny embrace,
All the laughter finds its place.
With every giggle, joy appears,
Wrapping us in the silliest cheers!

A Tangle of Light and Laughter

Tangled lights, oh what a mess,
Each knot a giggle, what a stress!
Uncle Joe has lost his shoe,
While dancing like an elf, it's true!

Reindeer games in the living room,
Cadbury eggs holding sweet perfume.
Tinsel strands cobweb the floor,
Hiding snacks behind the door!

Cousins tossing ornaments wide,
Landing on the cat with pride.
Chasing through wrapping paper spry,
Each clang and bang makes laughter fly!

In this tangle of joy and cheer,
We find the fun, it's crystal clear.
Each jolly moment, a twinkling spark,
Shining bright in the festive dark!

Sleigh Bells Ringing Through the Night

Sleigh bells jingle, what a tune,
Reindeer giggling at the moon.
Santa's lost his favorite hat,
It's on a dog, can you believe that?

Elves are dancing, making toys,
But tripping over all the noise.
A snowman with a carrot nose,
Complains about the chills, I suppose!

Hot cocoa spills upon the floor,
The cat's now plotting to explore.
With marshmallows flying high,
We've begun a chilly pie fight, oh my!

Magic twinkles in the air,
With silly socks, we're in despair.
Laughter echoes through the night,
Sleigh bells ringing, what a sight!

Canvas of Snowflakes and Stars

Snowflakes tumble, each unique,
A snowman squawks, 'It's me you seek!'
Dancing shadows, a funny sight,
Falling face-first in the white!

Stars are winking from above,
While squirrels plot a war of love.
A cat with mittens on its paws,
Chasing snowflakes with a pause.

Footprints lead to nowhere fast,
A lunchtime snowball fight—what a blast!
Hot cheddar cheese begins to melt,
On our noses, warmth is felt.

Blankets soft, we wrap around,
As giggles bounce upon the ground.
With cups of cheer, we toast the sky,
In this snowy tale, we all fly!

Cherished Moments of Radiant Cheer

Jingle bells and funny hats,
Grandma's dance makes everyone pat.
Tinsel tangled in the tree,
The dog just barked—so full of glee!

Cookies crumble, icing splats,
Painting spoons, we laugh, oh rats!
With laughter shared on every floor,
We can't find mom; she's at the store!

Presents wrapped with joyous flair,
What's inside? We just don't care!
Champagne bubbles and silly cheers,
With confetti flying through the years.

Memories twinkle, hearts aglow,
Amidst the chaos, love will grow.
In every giggle, every scream,
Together we weave, the perfect dream!

Frosty Mornings and Cozy Afternoons

Frosty mornings, oh what fun,
Chasing puppies, one by one.
January air bites at our nose,
As we march onward, full of eclairs and prose!

Cozy afternoons, warm and bright,
Marshmallows dive in tea, what a sight!
Quilts piled high, snug as a bug,
Telling stories, each little shrug.

A snowball rolls, it starts to grow,
Meets a snowman, with a friendly glow.
With funny hats and little feet,
They join the fun—a wintry treat!

Hot soup simmers, laughter flows,
With every sip, our cheer just grows.
So here's a toast, with spreading glee,
To frosty morns and warm jubilee!

Frosty Eves and Candlelight Glow

Frosty nights with snow so bright,
I slip and slide, a comical sight.
The candles dance in playful glee,
Who knew wax could waltz with me?

Eggnog spills, a cheerful mess,
With laughter more than I can guess.
The turkey's burnt, it's quite the scene,
Yet here we are, so merry and keen.

Stockings hung, I lost my shoe,
Now Santa's stuck—what's he to do?
With giggles muffling carol tunes,
We cheer for prances of festive goons.

Jingle bells on my pet cat's head,
He pounces, flips, then bounds to bed.
Our frosty eves are full of flair,
With funny tales we love to share.

Brimming Hearts and Holiday Cheer

A reindeer run that ends in snow,
Where holiday mishaps steal the show.
My granddad trips on flat-out pies,
While grandma hides her laughter's rise.

Pine scent wafts, and hats are askew,
We sing off-key, but it's our cue.
With mugs of cocoa, marshmallows fly,
A sweetened storm drifts through the sky.

Silly sweaters, bright and bold,
With tinsel strands that never grow old.
Inside jokes about the fruitcake,
Prompt giggles that we can't mistake.

When holiday lights flicker and blink,
We tumble into laughter, no time to think.
These moments spark joy, pure and clear,
With brimming hearts and holiday cheer.

In the Arms of Winter's Hold

Snowflakes whirl, a dance in the air,
I chased one down, what a funny scare!
With mittens stuck, I'm caught in glee,
 While snowmen come to life, oh me!

Winter's chill will sneak on in,
But hot cocoa's here, let the fun begin!
I spill it once, then twice, oh dear,
 Our laughter echoes far and near.

Shorts and flip-flops in the snow,
Frosty friends begin the show.
Wacky games with ice and cheer,
 Our winter wonderland is near.

As sleighs take flight on silent hills,
We ride and slide, our heartbeats thrill.
In winter's arms, we find our gold,
 With funny tales forever told.

Delighted Whispers of Christmas Past

Whispers soft from yesteryears,
Like ghostly giggles, tickles, and cheers.
Tinsel wrapped 'round granddad's nose,
He sneezed once, and off went the bows!

Pine cones crafted with joyful hands,
Gifts wrapped poorly—who understands?
Unruly fruitcake's tough to chew,
But around the table, we always knew.

Fuzzy socks and mistletoe pranks,
A line of laughter in rowdy ranks.
We share our tales with cheeky grins,
Recalling each goof and the joy it spins.

In holiday lights we find the past,
With secrets, giggles, that forever last.
Delighted whispers call us near,
As Christmas joy draws us all near.

The Reindeer's Flight Through Wishes

Up on the roof, oh what a sight,
Reindeer dancing with all their might!
They twirl and spin, in festive cheer,
While Santa laughs and drinks his beer.

The sleigh takes off with a hefty thud,
As Rudolph shouts, "We'll fly through mud!"
With jingle bells echoing far and wide,
They navigate the skies with a goofy glide.

Through clouds they zoom and whirl and twirl,
Each wish they carry gives a merry swirl.
"That one's for a bike!" a child does call,
But they drop it off right where the squirrels ball!

With laughter bursting from rooftop to street,
They spread pure joy and holiday treat.
Onward they go, with gusto and glee,
Making merry mischief 'neath the Christmas tree.

Songs of the North and Heart

In the North where snowmen sing,
Their carrots dance, oh what a fling!
With frosty cheeks and hats askew,
They hold a concert for me and you.

Snowflakes twirl like little stars,
While penguins skate with candy bars.
The laughter echoes through icy air,
As snowballs fly, with no care to spare.

A moose in a scarf leads the whole band,
While ice-fish jive and take a stand.
Each note a giggle, each chorus a cheer,
In this winter wonder, how could you fear?

So raise your mug, the fun will not cease,
With every giggle, we find our peace.
As joyful songs envelop the night,
We dance in the glow of soft, twinkling light.

Resplendent Moments in Midnight Blue

The stars sparkle bright in midnight hue,
As elves gather 'round, making crafts anew.
With bows and ribbons, they trip and they twist,
Each gift wrapped up with a clumsy fist.

Oh, watch as they tumble and giggle with glee,
Turning boxes into a festive spree.
With tape in their hair and glue on their nose,
They burst through the door, bright as a rose!

Midnight blue envelops the scene outside,
Where snowflakes wink and the quiet does bide.
But here inside, it's pure, wild delight,
With mischief and laughter, all through the night.

So raise your glass, let the fun just flow,
As dreams dance by like the soft, quiet snow.
In this merry chaos, our hearts intertwine,
Amidst wrapped-up moments, both funny and fine.

Dreams Draped in Holiday Splendor

On the twelfth day of Christmas, what a sight,
Dreams float by in pajamas tight!
With fairies giggling and popcorn strings,
Even the cat dons angel wings.

Wishes twinkle like lights on a tree,
As children dream of sugarplum glee.
With candy canes serving as magic wands,
They stir up giggles in joyful bands.

The dog jumps up in a jolly spree,
Chasing snowflakes like it's all free.
But oh, what's this? A slip and a slide,
With a bounce and a tumble, he's off for a ride!

This season of fun, full of surprise,
Wraps us in laughter, oh how time flies!
With dreams draped neatly in playful cheer,
We revel in warmth as the holiday's near.

Tinsel Dreams and Wishes Bright

In a land where snowmen wear hats too tall,
They dance on the street, oh what a brawl!
Jingle bells jingle, they're out of control,
Frosty's got moves that just steal the scroll.

Elves in the kitchen mix cocoa and cheer,
But one spills the marshmallows, oh dear, oh dear!
The reindeer are giggling, they can't seem to fly,
While Santa sneezes, oh my, oh my!

Ribbons and bows in a jumble so grand,
Cats try to climb them, they dream of a band.
Each twinkling light sings a song of delight,
As we laugh at the chaos, our hearts take flight.

So here's to the season with laughter so bright,
With jokes and mishaps that last through the night.
For nothing is sweeter than joy wrapped in fun,
As we toast to the madness, let laughter be done!

A Journey Through Frosted Fantasies

Through a forest of candy canes, we glide,
Frosty plays catch with a snow globe beside.
The tree bears a fruit that's bright candy red,
While squirrels wear scarves, they laugh till they're dead.

A sleigh pulled by puppies, not reindeer, oh no!
They zoom through the sky and put on quite a show.
With Santa in slippers and milk on his chin,
He's ready to cha-cha while we sip on gin.

The penguins are plotting to steal the whole pie,
While mice hold a party, oh how they can fly!
With giggles and murmurs, they dance on the floor,
Each nibble of cheese just makes them want more.

And when morning arrives, with wrapping in stacks,
It's chaos and laughter that fills all the cracks.
For a trip through this winter is a wild ride indeed,
With friends made of chocolate, it's fun that we need!

Mirth and Merriment in the Air

Under bright lights, the holiday cheer,
We find our great cousin, the jolly ones near.
They tumble and trip, wrapped up in the lights,
Presents explode, what a comical sight!

A cat in a hat steals a cupcake or two,
While kids giggle loudly, oh what can they do?
The snowflakes are falling, each one shaped like gold,
And stories of blunders are happily told.

The snowmen join in with their silly dance,
They wobble and wobble, oh what a chance!
Hot cocoa spills over as laughter unveils,
And chocolate keeps falling from jolly green trails.

So here we shall gather, the merry and bright,
With spirits so high in this magical night.
With giggles and whispers, we'll sing tunes of glee,
For mirth is the gift we prefer with our tea!

Threads of Gold and Silver Wishes

Threading through dreams with a glittery thread,
A llama in pjs ate all that we spread.
While gingerbread men are plotting their flight,
They'll take off like rockets in the soft, pale night.

Santa's got hiccups and says 'ho ho why?'
As elves laugh aloud and the reindeer all sigh.
Tinsel's on trees but it's stuck on the cat,
He prances around like a fluffy acrobat.

With snowflakes that giggle and twirl in the breeze,
The joy in the season brings everyone ease.
On the rooftop, the antics of squirrels abound,
As snowmen pull pranks and their laughs echo round.

So let's raise a toast to the silly and bright,
For laughter and wishes will fill up the night.
With threads spun from joy that will never come loose,
We'll wear all the smiles, it's the best kind of use!

The Spirit of Giving and Receiving

In a land of wrapped presents and glee,
Santa's lost his list, oh me, oh my!
What will he do? Will he flee?
A carrot for Rudolph? Just a sly try!

Elves are giggling, their cheeks all aglow,
While tripping on candy canes left in the snow.
Is that a reindeer stuck in a bow?
Guess there's still time for the merriment flow!

A present for Fido, or was it for me?
Oh, who can remember after all this spree!
Tangled in ribbons, so giddy, so free,
The cookies are gone, just crumbs, you see!

But laughter and joy, that's the best gift,
With cookies and cocoa, let spirits uplift!
A wink and a chuckle, Santa's clever rift,
As we hold tight to this mirthful shift!

A Dance of Elves in Winter's Hold

In a workshop bustling, they jive and sway,
Elves in their slippers, they dance through the fray.
With toys flying high in a laugh-out-loud way,
They trip over tinsel, oh what a display!

Singing carols off-key, what a merry sight,
Spinning 'round snowmen, what pure delight!
One trips on a sled, oh what a fright,
Yet up they bounce, with giggles so bright!

Cocoa spills everywhere, the mugs taking flight,
As snowflakes pirouette in the crisp, starry night.
Elves on the ceiling, such a curious sight,
But it's all in good fun, spreading cheer, that's right!

With ribbons all tangled and giggles galore,
A dance by the fire, let's ask for no more!
Wishing you laughter, let humor restore,
As we spin through the season, a joy to explore!

Starlit Paths and Frosty Trails

On a snowy night, with stars so bright,
We venture outside, in sheer delight.
With hot cocoa mugs and snowballs in flight,
We stumble and fumble, oh what a sight!

Snowmen appear, with noses so round,
But one's looking grumpy, he frowns on the ground.
'Who made me like this?' a comical sound,
As we all burst out laughing, joyfully unbound!

As the frost bites our toes, we tumble with cheer,
The reindeer are prancing, but they seem a bit queer.
"Can they dance like us?"—it's perfectly clear,
They'd step on each other to join us down here!

With starlit paths and frosty trails wide,
We'll remember these moments with laughter and pride.
So cuddle up close, enjoy the sly ride,
Through whimsical nights, let joy be our guide!

Heartstrings Tied in Red and Green

In Grandma's garland, there's a story to share,
A missing sock warns of a cat's despair.
Kittens in tinsel, oh how they ensnare,
Tangled in laughter with a whimsical flair!

With gifts piled high, there's so much to see,
When uncle shows up in a bow and a bee.
"What do you mean? It's festive to me!"
While dodging Aunt Mabel with cookies for free!

Ribbons now dancing, on doggy's bright tail,
He prances in circles, the king of the veil.
With each little tug, we all can't curtail,
The laughter that echoes, amid the details!

So gather around, let the stories ignite,
With heartstrings all tied in colors so bright.
For laughter is magic, our purest delight,
Through red and green dreams, our hearts take flight!

Whispers of Yuletide Wishes

Santa's sleigh ran out of gas,
Rudolph's stuck; he can't pass.
Elves on strike, they need a raise,
Holiday fun in silly ways!

Frosty lost his carrot nose,
Now he sneezes—who knows those?
Gingerbread men in a dash,
Look out for the big fat splash!

Jingle bells come with a twist,
Every toy makes a funny list.
Socks are missing, where's the pair?
Maybe with the reindeer fair!

Twinkling lights string up in style,
Underneath there's doggone guile.
Hoping snow will fall on time,
To catch our giggles in a rhyme!

Echoes in the Winter Night

Up on the roof, a clatter's loud,
Could it be Santa, or a cat proud?
Whiskers twitch in the frosty air,
That crunch is just a wild bear!

Hot cocoa spills in frantic glee,
Marshmallows float like a birthday spree.
With a sip, I start to float,
Guess this year, I'm a gourmet goat!

Snowmen gather for a dance,
Winter's ball—a jolly chance!
Slipping, sliding, down the hill,
Round and round, what a thrill!

Under stars that twinkle bright,
Elves are partying with delight.
While I'm here, wrapped in a quilt,
They're busy brewing fun, no guilt!

Tinsel Tides of Hope

Tinsel drapes from every eave,
Joking 'bout what we believe.
Maybe Santa's just a guy,
With a sleigh too low to fly!

Eggnog's flowing, time to cheer,
A spoon or two, let's make it clear!
Cookies signed with kids' best luck,
Oops! One dropped—oh, what the muck!

Gifts wrapped tightly, oh what fun,
Last year's present's come undone.
Cat's found comfort in the box,
He's turned our gift into a fox!

Lights are twinkling, but one's gone,
Now my heart's doing a con!
Hoping for a festive spark,
Next year, maybe less of a lark!

Wreaths of Warmth and Wonder

Plum pudding pops like a dynamite,
Jolly faces, quite the sight!
Grandpa's telling tales with flair,
Santa's wisdom shined with care.

Warm hugs shared 'round the tree,
Tangled lights? A laughing spree.
A snowball fight turns into snow,
And Grandma's chasing them, oh no!

Pine cones fall, and we must dodge,
With each thud, we merrily lodge.
Ho ho ho! The laughter spills,
Through the night, it joyfully thrills!

So here's to dreams, all silly and bright,
With every gaffe, there's pure delight.
Cheer and laughter, that's the key,
In each home, may joy run free!

Sweet Sips of Cocoa and Cheer

In mugs so round and stout,
Marshmallows dance about.
Stirring spoons take flight,
Cocoa's warmth brings light.

The cat leaps for a taste,
A splash, oh what a waste!
Chocolate on his nose,
In winter's silly pose.

Snowflakes fall, a sight so grand,
Puppies prance in snowy land.
They tumble, chase, then roll,
Ending up in a cocoa bowl!

So grab your cup, let's cheer,
As laughter fills the air near.
With cocoa sips and giggles sweet,
This cozy joy cannot be beat.

Sprigs of Holly and Tangled Vines

Holly jolly on the door,
But the cat knocked it to the floor.
Tangled vines and glittered mess,
We laugh at this sweet Christmas stress.

Lights twinkle with a funky twist,
Each bulb a funny little twist.
Unraveled strands from head to toe,
Who knew trees could be so woe?

Children giggle in the night,
As they chase the dog in flight.
With ribbons flying overhead,
The holiday cheer is widespread!

So deck the halls with sticky glue,
And let the good times grow anew.
For in this merry, joyful scene,
We find the fun in all that's seen.

Wishes Carried on the Winter Wind

Whispers of wishes in the breeze,
Twirling snowflakes dance with ease.
A wish for socks that fit just right,
And snowmen with a little bite!

Santa's reindeer lose their way,
They prance and dance in bright array.
One slipped on ice, oh what a sight,
He landed safe, in a snowball fight!

As carolers sing out loud and clear,
The dog joins in with a holiday cheer.
His howl is off, but who's to mind,
In this merry season, joy's what we find!

Let wishes drift like snowflakes new,
Float on the wind, and bring delight too.
For every laugh this season brings,
Are the sweetest of all winter things.

Threads of Joy in Weaving Time

Weaving joy with threads so bright,
Colorful mischief, pure delight.
Grandma's knitting goes awry,
A scarf for a squirrel caught up high!

The knitting needles click and clack,
As playful kittens plot their attack.
Little paws in yarn they dive,
Creating chaos, yet feeling alive!

When mittens turn to silly hats,
And snowballs fly with giggly spats.
We weave our dreams in festive cheer,
With laughter bound to draw us near.

So gather 'round and share the fun,
As we count down and each day run.
For every stitch and every line,
Holds a memory, sweet and fine.

A Symphony of Peaceful Nights

The cat dons a hat, quite absurd,
Chasing shadows, not a sound heard.
The elves have mixed up all the toys,
Gifts for girls are now for boys.

Old Santa's sleigh is stuck in a tree,
He's yelling for help, quite desperately.
The reindeer are laughing, taking their time,
On the roof, they lounge, sipping warm thyme.

There's eggnog spilled on the kitchen floor,
The dog thinks it's his, he's back for more.
Grandma's baking cookies, what a mess,
With flour on her nose, she looks quite blessed.

As midnight strikes, the neighbors can hear,
A chorus of carolers, not so clear.
With off-key tunes, they bring such cheer,
But the cats hide away, they don't want near.

Threads of Light in Twinkling Eyes

A squirrel's found a shiny bauble,
Thinking it's food, but it's just trouble.
The lights flicker, a disco scene,
Peaceful nights aren't quite what they seem.

There's a snowman wearing a scarf too long,
He trips and falls, it doesn't feel wrong.
The kids are busy with snowball fights,
While the dog burrows, what a silly sight!

In the distance, laughter echoes loud,
The whole town gathers, feeling proud.
Giggling children covered in snow,
Making snow angels, all in a row.

The moon shines bright above the fun,
As the year ends, they all feel spun.
With warmth and joy, they dance till late,
Even the cat has joined their fate.

Joyous Echoes in the Frosted Air

A penguin in a sweater, what a sight,
Slipping and sliding, oh what delight!
Hot cocoa spills, and giggles erupt,
On a frosty slope, a sledder's abrupt.

The lights on the tree are tangled and bright,
A bunny hops in, causing a fright.
In the kitchen, a pie is on fire,
The smell is funny, oh my, oh dire!

Christmas carols sung out of key,
The dog joins in, oh can't you see?
A choir of giggles fills up the night,
In the wintry glow, hearts feel so light.

With scarves and mittens, they rush outside,
Snowballs are flying, not one can hide.
Laughter is shared, all woes disappear,
As they revel together, this time of year.

Treading on the Tinsel Path

The cat sits proud atop the tree,
With tinsel draped, looking quite free.
The ornaments wobble, they're not secure,
As he leaps down, it's laughter for sure!

There's a child in a box, thinking it's grand,
Waving to Santa as if it's all planned.
The dog steals a present, running away,
Barking with joy, "Is it Christmas Day?"

The snowflakes tickle as they land on noses,
While dad's in the kitchen, baking some poses.
His apron's too tight, it's a comedy show,
He burns the cookies, oh no, oh no!

Yet still the joy swells, filling the air,
As the clock chimes, friends gather to share.
With laughter and cheer, they all raise a cup,
In this merry chaos, they're never downed up.

Milton Keynes UK
Ingram Content Group UK Ltd.
UKHW021844151124
451262UK00014B/1301